FRANCHI
FEELS RIGHT

COOKBOOK
GAME ON

MARETTI
EDITORE

FRANCHI FOOD ACADEMY
COOKBOOK

Publishing Director
Manfredi Nicolò Maretti

Editor in Chief
Maria Paola Poponi

Graphic Design
Maretti Editore

© Maretti Editore 2022
© Franchi Food Academy 2022

ISBN 978-88-9397-056-3

SUMMARY

INDEX OF RECIPES

STARTER

FIRST COURSE

Trentingrana tagliolini, venison stock and bread sauce	DEER	51
Fusilli with rosemary, pheasant and orange zest	PHEASANT	53
Wild boar cappelletti with cheese fondue, truffle and cherry	WILD BOAR	55
Tortelli stuffed with mallard	MALLARD	57
Wild boar spaghetti carbonara	WILD BOAR	59
Spelt pasta with venison carbonara	DEER	61
Partridge and savoy cabbage risotto	PARTRIDGE	63
Casareccia with venison and porcini mushrooms	FALLOW DEER	65
Cappellacci with venison and Mediterranean flavors	ROE DEER	67
Wild turkey and spring risotto	TURKEY	69
Baked pasta with venison sausage	DEER	71
Wild boar fazzoletto	WILD BOAR	73
Cappellacci pasta with pheasant, peppers and crusco	PHEASANT	75
Fisarmoniche, mouflon small meatballs and eggplants	MOUFLON	77
Spaghetti with game ragù and burrata	GAME MEAT	79
Risotto with chicory and hare	HARE	81
Risotto strawberries and partridges		

SECOND COURSE

Herb crusted venison crown roast	ROE DEER	83
Chamois cutlets	CHAMOIS	85
Elk chili	ELK	87
Hare's stew	HARE	89
Venison tomahawk with florets salad	ROE DEER	91
Venison tartare with October scent	DEER	93
Wild boar BBQ ribs	WILD BOAR	95
Wood pigeon, chicory, red fruit apples and halzenut sauce	WOOD PIGEON	97
Sika carpaccio	DEER	99
Venison pastrami, chamomile mayonnaise, pickled cherries	FALLOW DEER	101
Venison burgers with poplars	DEER	103
Capercaillie with potatoes, onion cream and blueberry sauce	CAPERCAILLIE	105
Crispy hare confit	HARE	107
Salmi of duck	DUCK	109
Tempura turkey tenders with ponzu	TURKEY	111
Roasted venison with Béarnaise sauce	DEER	113
Wild boar tenderloin with squash, apples and black kale	WILD BOAR	115
Air compressor roasted duck	DUCK	117

PREFACE

Let's start this new culinary chapter by Franchi Food Academy with a semantics question. You're probably wondering, "Semantics? This is a cookbook, what does studying the meaning of language ever have to do with it?!" Well, now we will surprise you a little, showing that in this particular case it has something to do with it. Just like cooking moves senses and feelings, the same goes for words, which are able to move mountains and knowing the meaning within can make the difference between mere "hearsay" and a real awareness.

So, the question we ask is this: what does *sustainability* mean?

Nowadays we can say that this word is really on everyone's lips and more and more often it comes out among the *vast sea* of texts, articles, interviews and talk shows of current affairs, but who knows if whoever pronounces it really knows its meaning.

This word derives from the Latin verb "sustĭneo, sustinēre", that is to support, help, but also nourish, prolong over time. And *this* is the key to the concept: time. Sustainability means ensuring that the needs of the present generation are met, without compromising the ability of future generations to achieve their own. Produce and Preserve.

We know, they are "big" concepts and yes, perhaps even a little too serious for a simple recipe book... you were expecting just recipes, creativity and healthy fun! But here's the thing, we could say the plot twist. Today we reveal that even you, perhaps without even realizing, while delighting between a roe deer tartare and a fine wild boar sauce, have adopted a *sustainable* behavior.

In fact, our food system is unfortunately primarily responsible for climate change, from the production of CO_2 to the phenomenon of *food wasting*, and the choices we make at the table not only may but *do make* a difference. Game meat is one of them.

What is sustainable if not the wild? An animal that is born in nature, lives free, is taken without stress and for this reason is rich in taste and nutrients and low in fat. This wonderful raw material is not only healthy, but versatile, it lends itself to various preparations and fights "naturally" food waste, because you can taste practically everything from the wild game. In addition, its being rarer than normal, contributes to decrease the annual consumption of meat of everyone.

Franchi Food Academy is also this: a project aimed at enhancing game and transmitting its quality, safety, control and transparency. Without ever forgetting the fun, flavors and conviviality. In short, be sustainable with taste!

In this book you will find as usual 52 recipes, one a week, to juggle in the kitchen and share with friends. And if when you taste the first bite, you get an extra smile... that's right, because you're really *doing* something sustainable.

DISCOVERING
THE CHEFS

MATTEO CODIGNOLI
ITALY

At only 19, he is one of the youngest chefs in the Marche region, graduated from the Hotel School of Piobbico and with a passion for cooking that has conquered him since he was a child. One of his first achievements was the award of the competition Bosco in Tavola, with a dish that exalted the typical products of his territory. We do not know what the future holds, but surely this job can give him many other satisfactions, such as working around the world to explore new dishes.

ROBERTO DORMICCHI
ITALY

He loves to define himself as a chef and more. Passionate about sports and outdoor activities, teacher of a Marche cooking school, he lives a few kilometers from Acqualagna, the homeland of truffles, and has been in the culinary sector for about twenty years. He collaborates with numerous restaurants and colleagues, including Mauro Uliassi, whose influence has marked a real leap in quality in his professional growth. He was among the first to join the Franchi Food Academy network.

MICHAEL HUNTER
CANADA

Professional chef and lover of the outdoors, in 2015 he opens the acclaimed Antler restaurant in Toronto and in 2020 he publishes his first cookbook *The Hunter Chef Cookbook*, which wins the second prize of the Taste Canada Cookbook Awards, in the fall of 2021. Michael has been a proud Franchi hunter for 10 years.

GABRIEL JONSSON
SWEDEN

Love for food, hunting, fishing and days in contact with nature – that's how Gabriel describes himself. A dreamer, who in 2019 chose to change his life, leaving a secure job in the construction industry and dedicating himself to his greatest passion: cooking. The same year he participates and wins the edition of Swedish Master Chef, opening the doors to a life that until then was just a dream.

IRIS ROSSI
ITALY

Daughter of restaurateurs and hunters, she literally grew up in the kitchen among the traditional family recipes, which she loves to creatively revisit in a modern way. Also, thanks to this passion, she is one of the founders of Franchi Food Academy, which she has been carrying forward with enthusiasm from day one.

STEFANO MARINUCCI
ITALY

Author of numerous articles in specialized magazines and books in the sector, lecturer at Carpigiani Gelato University, over the years he has been the protagonist of several television programs on national networks. In 2014 he won the gold medal in the World Culinary Cup, thanks to a salt sculpture. Dog lover by passion, he keeps up the family culinary tradition, with choreographic dishes based on game.

DISCOVERING
THE CHEFS

ILENIA ROSSI
ITALY

Passion for cooking is a matter of DNA. Born into a family of restaurateurs and hunters, she attended the Hotel School and what she studied was a confirmation that cooking is her vocation. The internship at a famous fish restaurant in Pesaro province is the key to her training. There she learnt plenty of preparations and skills that she brings back today in her game recipes.

DARIUSH LOLAIY
NEW ZEALAND

Multi-award-winning chef and cookbook author, hunter and co-owner at Cazador, one of the New Zealand's longest running restaurants. Dariush's specialty is serving game and free-range meats, and fresh, local produce with an emphasis on ethically sourced ingredients and minimal waste. At Cazador, classic, hands-on cooking techniques are used to create simple, sophisticated dishes using local, quality ingredients.

EDOARDO SBARAGLIA
ITALY

Born in 1994, a chef from Rome but of French origin, began his training at Magnolia (1 Michelin star). However, it was in Edinburgh, in the Martin Wishart Restaurant (1 Michelin star) that his passion for game was born. Back in Rome he worked in the Pagliaccio restaurant (2 Michelin stars), where he learned to blend different culinary traditions. Today he is the chef of the Brado restaurant, where he combines the precious game meat with the fruits of the forest, all in a natural and sustainable way.

VILLI TOSI
NEW ZEALAND

Growing up on a farm in New Zealand, the outdoors runs through his veins. Fishing and hunting are for him a real lifestyle, in which ethics and respect for nature are key values. Hence, Villi came up with the idea of filming some of his adventures and sharing them, with hunters and not only, on his Wild Meat Hunter NZ channel. Tidbits of experiences, from the moment of going out to the end of the day, which inevitably ends around a table, with a new game recipe.

WADE TRUONG
USA

Lifelong Virginian, he is a self-taught chef and hunter, who combines a passion for the table with a deep sense of gratitude towards the environment and the natural riches offered to us, to be protected and safeguarded. For Wade, every meal should be cherished and celebrated, meaningful and conscious, as a reminder of who we are, where we come from and where we are going.

NUTRITIONAL VALUES
#TASTERIGHT

VENISON
CARBOHYDRATE	0 g
PROTEIN	36,08 g
FAT	3,93 g
ENERGY	190 kcal

WILD BOAR
CARBOHYDRATE	0 g
PROTEIN	27,8 g
FAT	4,3 g
ENERGY	157 kcal

HARE
CARBOHYDRATE	0 g
PROTEIN	32,88 g
FAT	3,5 g
ENERGY	172 kcal

TURKEY
CARBOHYDRATE	0 g
PROTEIN	28,81 g
FAT	2,06 g
ENERGY	139 kcal

DUCK
CARBOHYDRATE	0 g
PROTEIN	23,38 g
FAT	11,15 g
ENERGY	200 kcal

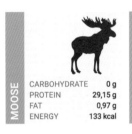

MOOSE
CARBOHYDRATE	0 g
PROTEIN	29,15 g
FAT	0,97 g
ENERGY	133 kcal

QUAIL
CARBOHYDRATE	0 g
PROTEIN	25 g
FAT	14,04 g
ENERGY	226 kcal

GOOSE
CARBOHYDRATE	0 g
PROTEIN	25,06 g
FAT	21,83 g
ENERGY	304 kcal

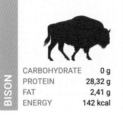

BISON
CARBOHYDRATE	0 g
PROTEIN	28,32 g
FAT	2,41 g
ENERGY	142 kcal

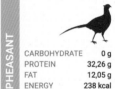

PHEASANT
CARBOHYDRATE	0 g
PROTEIN	32,26 g
FAT	12,05 g
ENERGY	238 kcal

STORE BOUGHT MEAT

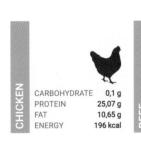

CHICKEN
CARBOHYDRATE	0,1 g
PROTEIN	25,07 g
FAT	10,65 g
ENERGY	196 kcal

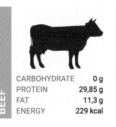

BEEF
CARBOHYDRATE	0 g
PROTEIN	29,85 g
FAT	11,3 g
ENERGY	229 kcal

PORK
CARBOHYDRATE	0 g
PROTEIN	27,69 g
FAT	10,5 g
ENERGY	211 kcal

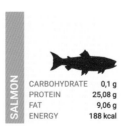

SALMON
CARBOHYDRATE	0,1 g
PROTEIN	25,08 g
FAT	9,06 g
ENERGY	188 kcal

(Average vaules based on 100 g of portion)
Source: US Department of Agricolture, Agricoltural Research Service

WILD GAME MEAT

On the nutritional level, the composition of game meat in terms of macronutrients and micronutrients is interesting. Regarding the scope of macronutrients, the literature suggests, in fact, a high protein content of high biological value and, at the same time, a restrained quantity of the lipid component with a valid composition as regards the profile of fatty acids (Corradini et al., 2022).

In detail, game meat is a good source of essential amino acids, which, as the name suggests, are necessary for the human body, which is not able to synthesize them independently. Furthermore, by analyzing the ratio of omega 3 / omega 6 polyunsaturated fatty acids present in game meat, it is positive for the human body.

On micronutrients, which unlike carbohydrates, proteins and lipids do not provide energy, but are equally important for the proper functioning of our body, it is interesting to note that game meat is a source of multiple minerals and vitamins such as iron, zinc and vitamin B12 (Viganò et al., 2021).

Finally, a recent editorial of the scientific journal "Foods" (Branciari & Ranucci, 2022) reports how other nutritional factors of game meat, such as bioactive compounds with antihypertensive properties, should be taken into account. In this context, the editorial cites a study that shows that the inhibitory activities of the angiotensin conversion enzyme I (ACE) are higher in digested game meat compared to some farmed meat.

The nutritional scenario briefly described implies a look of interest towards game meat, a healthy food when considered within a broader framework of lifestyle and dietary models such as the Mediterranean one. However, always ask your doctor for personalized dietary advice.

Silvio Barbero

Vice-president of the Pollenzo University of Gastronomic Sciences Food Lab

VENISON TARTARE WITH CHIPS
SOY YOLK AND TRUFFLE

Serves
4

Time
20'

Calories
244 Kcal

Wine
Barbera D'Alba DOC

Difficulty
Low

Game
Roe deer

Chef
Edoardo Sbaraglia

Run
M 22' F 31'

Preparation

Put the egg yolks in a container and let them flavor in the soy sauce for 18 h. Then drain the egg yolks, using a whisk to make a smooth mixture.

Finely chop the red turnip and fry it in sunflower oil to obtain crispy chips.

Clean the loin from the filaments and mince it with a knife to form a tartare. Dress the tartare with oil, salt, and pepper, mix everything in a bowl and plate it, using a mold.

Place the red turnip chips and the truffle finely sliced on top. Using a pastry bag, decorate the plate with the soy yolk and garnish with fresh sprouts.

Ingredients

G 400 venison loin
G 125 red turnip
G 20 black truffle
mL 500 soy sauce
N 4 egg yolks
Fresh sprouts to taste
Salt and pepper to taste
Extra virgin olive oil to taste
Sunflower oil to taste

VENISON
BRESAOLA

Serves
4

Time
1 month

Calories
278 Kcal

Wine
Alta Langa Spumante Rosato
DOCG

Difficulty
Medium

Game
Deer

Chef
Villi Tosi

Run
M 25' F 35'

Preparation

Make sure your meat has most of the fat and all of the sinew removed. Bresaola is supposed to be lean.

Mix the salt, sugar, spices and dried herbs together. Rub maple syrup thoroughly over all of the meat and then massage the combined dry mix into the meat, so it is well coated.

Put the meat into a plastic zip-lock bag or container with a sealed lid. Put it in the refrigerator. Cure this for 12 days, turning the meat over once a day. Pour off any liquid that accumulates, and redistribute the spices as needed. If the meat is small, adjust your cure days to half.

After 12 days remove meat and rinse off the spices under cold water and pat dry with paper towels.

If you know how to truss the meat, then do so and hang in a chamber or chiller at 10 °C (50 °F) for 2 weeks. The venison has to lose the 30% of weight.

After 2 weeks remove and thinly slice the meat and enjoy with soft cheese and crackers.

Ingredients

Kg 1 venison loin
N 2 tbsp Kosher salt
N 3 tbsp sugar
N 1 tbsp maple syrup
N 2 tbsp smoked paprika
N 1 tbsp dried marjoram
N 2 tbsp dried sage
N 2 tbsp ground black pepper

SMOKED HEART
CHARCUTERIE

Serves
4

Time
1 h 30'

Calories
210 Kcal

Wine
Sforzato di Valtellina DOCG

Difficulty
Low

Game
Deer

Chef
Michael Hunter

Run
M 19' F 26'

Preparation

Add half the water to a pot with the salt, sugar, bay leaves, thyme and cloves. Bring to a boil.

Add the rest of the cold water and a handful of ice cubes to cool it down. When the liquid is cold, place the heart in a container and pour the liquid over it. Keep in the fridge for at least 12 h or overnight. If you want, you can cure the heart up to a week before smoking it.

Set the smoker to 110 °C (230 °F) and smoke until the internal temperature is 80 °C (160 °F). The heart can be served hot or cold, cut thin. If you don't have a smoker, the heart can be slow roasted in the oven.

You can serve it on crackers with aioli and top with mustard and pickled onions as decoration.

Ingredients

N 1 heart (approx. G 500)
L 2 water
G 140 salt
G 50 sugar
N 2 bay leaves
N 2 sprigs thyme
Pinch of whole cloves to taste
Ice cubes to taste
Crackers to taste
Mustard to taste
Aioli to taste
Pickled onions to taste

PAN ROASTED QUAIL
DUCK FAT CARROT AND SORREL

Serves
4

Time
2 h

Calories
295 Kcal

Wine
Sicilia DOC Chardonnay

Difficulty
Medium

Game
Quail

Chef
Dariush Lolaiy

Run
M 27' F 37'

Preparation

Clean the quails and cut them in half. Season the quail liberally with salt and pepper. Sear them and season liberally with salt and pepper.

Make a marinade by mixing the pimentón with the cumin, minced garlic clove and oil. Coat the quail in the marinade.

Cook 300 g of chopped and peeled carrot in the carrot juice until it is very soft. Strain the carrots and reserve the juice. Blend into a puree, and adjust consistency by adding the juice back to the puree. Adjust seasoning with salt.

Meanwhile, cut the remaining carrots in half lengthwise. Gently cook the carrot halves in the duck fat with the whole cumin seeds until just cooked. This works well sous vide or could be done in a shallow tray in a medium hot oven 180 °C (356 °F).

Preheat the oven to 200 °C (392 °F), cook the quail on a hot pan for about 2' each side, then finish for 3' in the oven. The meat should be just cooked through – use a digital thermometer to test the temperature close to the bone, and it should be 60 °C (140 °F) at the thickest part. Rest the birds for 5'.

To serve, spoon the carrot puree onto the plate, dress the sorrel with olive oil and salt. Lay a duck fat carrot on the plate and arrange the quail on top of the carrot. Drizzle the resting juices from the quail back over the meat.

Ingredients

N 4 quail, spatchcocked
N 6 carrots
mL 500 carrot juice
N 3 tsp pimentón de la Vera (smoked paprika)
N 1 tbsp ground cumin
N 1 clove garlic, minced
N 1 splash extra virgin olive oil
N 2 tbsp of duck fat
N 1 tsp cumin seeds
N 8 sorrel leaves

SALTED VENISON
WITH CAULIFLOWER AND WILD ASPARAGUS

Serves
4

Time
30'

Calories
386 Kcal

Wine
Trentino Marzemino DOC

Difficulty
Low

Game
Roe deer

Chef
Edoardo Sbaraglia

Run
M 35' F 48'

Preparation

To start, degrease the leg, once clean, open it as if it were to be stuffed and sprinkle it with finely chopped aromatic herbs. At this point roll it up as if it were a roast and tie it well.

Put sugar and salt in a bowl and mix well.

In another large container place a rack, which will be used to drain the liquids during salting, and lay the leg. Then cover it with sugar and salt and leave it in the refrigerator for 48-72 h covered.

Then wash it with cold running water, so as to eliminate salt residues.

Clean cauliflowers and asparagus and blanch in water and salt. Then subject them to thermal shock by immersing them in water and ice.

Combine the yogurt with the spices and fenugreek to obtain a sauce with a pungent and slightly spicy flavor.

Blend a bit of the cauliflower so that you get a cream and leave the other bit as a whole.

Make the dish by finely cutting the meat and then, playing with the colors, place cauliflowers and asparagus and garnish with the cream.

You can store the rest of the meat in a vacuum refrigerator.

Ingredients

Kg 2 boneless roe deer leg
N 2 colored cauliflowers
(purple, yellow or white)
G 150 wild asparagus
G 150 low-fat yogurt
G 18 fenugreek
Kg 3 fine salt
Kg 1 sugar
G 250 aromatic herbs

WILD BOAR
OLIVES ASCOLANA

Serves 4	**Time** 20'	**Calories** 366 Kcal	**Wine** Offida Rosso DOCG
Difficulty Low	**Game** Wild boar	**Chef** Michael Hunter	**Run** M 35' F 46'

Preparation

Mix all of the meat with the parmesan cheese, salt, pepper, chili and nutmeg well to combine.

Cut the olives in half and generously stuff the olives with the meat. Squeeze in your hand tight and place on a tray.

Heat the oil to 175 °C (350 °F) in a large pan or pot.

Roll the olives in the flour, previously seasoned with salt and oil, then egg then into the bread crumbs to coat.

Gentle drop the breaded olives into the hot oil and fry until deep golden in color about 2-3'. Cut one olive in half to make sure the meat is cooked before removing all of them.

Serve with a slice of lemon and fried herbs.

Ingredients

G 150 ground wild boar meat
N 20 green olives
G 10 grated parmesan
N 2 eggs beaten
G 130 flour
G 130 bread crumbs (Italian style not panko)
L 2 vegetable oil for frying
Pinch of nutmeg
Pinch of chili flakes
Salt and pepper to taste
Lemon and fried herbs to taste

BAGEL WITH VENISON CARPACCIO
AVOCADO AND RICOTTA

👤 **Serves**
4

🎨 **Time**
1 h 10'

🔥 **Calories**
650 Kcal

🍷 **Wine**
Frascati Superiore
Riserva DOCG

⭐ **Difficulty**
Medium

🦌 **Game**
Fallow deer

👤 **Chef**
Iris Rossi

🏃 **Run**
M 59' F 81'

Preparation

Dissolve the yeast and honey in the water, at room temperature.

Sift the flour with the salt and gradually add the water until it forms a smooth dough, then add the anise seeds. Knead vigorously for 10'.

Form the dough into a ball and leave to rise, covered with cling film, until it doubles in size.

Divide the dough into 4 pieces of similar weight and roll into balls. Make a hole in the center with your fingers to form a bagel shape. Widen the hole so that 2-3 fingers can pass through it.

Place the bagels on a baking sheet lined with well-floured parchment paper, cover, and leave to rise until doubled in size.

Bake at 180 °C (356 °F) in a preheated static oven for about 20' then leave to cool.

Peel the avocado and blend the pulp after seasoning with salt, pepper, and oil.

Trim the loin of any sinew and silver skin and slice very thinly to make the carpaccio.

Cut the bagels in half, arrange the carpaccio, avocado, ricotta and previously toasted pistachios on the bottom half, season with salt and pepper and place the other half of the bagel on top.

Ingredients

G 400 venison loin
G 450 "0" flour
mL 300 water
G 6 fresh brewer's yeast
N 2 tbsp of honey
N 2 tsp of salt
N 1 tbsp of baking soda
N 1 avocado
G 200 mixed ricotta cheese
Pistachios to taste
Anise seeds to taste
Extra virgin olive oil to taste
Salt and pepper to taste

DUCK PROSCIUTTO

Serves
4

Time
15'

Calories
157 Kcal

Wine
Franciacorta Rosè DOCG

Difficulty
Low

Game
Duck

Chef
Michael hunter

Run
M 14' F 20'

Preparation

Rub salt over the duck meat and skin and place in a Tupperware or vacuum container. Let rest in a cool place or in the refrigerator. After two days, turn the duck breasts upside down in the container and let dry for two more days.

Remove the salt with the aid of cold running water. Hang the breasts in a cool, dark place for 1-2 weeks until the meat is well seasoned. The inside should be soft but not sticky.

Finely slice the duck breasts and serve with pickles and mustard along with some fresh bread or croutons.

Ingredients

G 500 duck breasts
G 65 salt
Bread to taste
Pickles to taste
Mustard to taste

QUAIL HEARTS
WITH POMEGRANATE AND PINE NUTS

Serves 4	**Time** 45'	**Calories** 436 Kcal	**Wine** Marsala DOC Vergine o Soleras
Difficulty Medium	**Game** Quail	**Chef** Dariush Lolaiy	**Run** M 40' F 54'

Preparation

Marinate the hearts with the ground spices, garlic and olive oil. Season well with salt.

Peel and cut the celeriac into small cubes. Cook in milk until very soft. Blend the celeriac to make a smooth puree, add the milk if it is too thick. Mix the celeriac and the labneh in equal quantities, adjust seasoning to taste.

Cook the pine nuts in butter until golden brown, strain and reserve the butter for cooking. Season the hearts with sea salt.

Set a heavy-based pan to high heat. Add ½ tsp fat and the hearts. Season with salt as the hearts caramelize on one side. Resist the urge to move them around for about 15", until they are nicely caramelized.

Toss the hearts in the pan to cook on the other side, and cook for a further 20". Add the vinegar and toss the hearts again. Allow the vinegar to reduce for a few seconds, then add the sherry and let it reduce for another 5". Remove the pan from the heat.

Add the pomegranate molasses and toss the pan so it coats the hearts. Pour the hearts and sauce into a bowl to stop the cooking.

Spoon the puree onto a plate, top with the hearts and sauce. Sprinkle pine nuts on top of the hearts and garnish with finely chopped chives.

Ingredients

G 300 quail hearts
G 100 labneh (strained yogurt)
G 50 pine nuts
G 30 unsalted butter
G 30 chives
mL 30 extra virgin olive oil
mL 150 milk
mL 30 sherry vinegar
mL 30 olorosso vinegar
mL 80 pomegranate molasses
N 1 celeriac
N 1 tbs ground cumin
N 1 tbs ground coriander
N 1 sliced clove of garlic

BRAISED VENISON
WITH RED BERRIES AND FRIED CECINA

Serves
4

Time
40'

Calories
470 Kcal

Wine
Teroldego Rotaliano DOC

Difficulty
Low

Game
Deer

Chef
Edoardo Sbaraglia

Run
M 43' F 59'

Preparation

Clean the venison fillet then sear in a frying pan with a little oil to "seal" it. Allow to cool and then place in a vacuum pouch with the wine, red berries, celery, carrot and onion. Cook the meat in the pouch for 12 h in a steam oven at a temperature of 73 °C (163 °F).

While the braised meat is cooking, make the cecina, or chickpea flatbread. Place the chickpea flour, salt, olive oil and water in a bowl and mix well. Once the dough is smooth, roll out to a thickness of 5-6 cm and cut out a rectangle of about 4×10 cm. Heat the vegetable oil in a pan and as soon as it is ready, fry the flatbread.

Once the meat is cooked, remove it from the vacuum pouch and blend the rest of the ingredients together, reduce this mixture in a saucepan until it becomes a smooth, thick sauce.

Serve the sauce over the braised meat, accompanied by the fried cecina.

Ingredients

G 500 fillet of venison
G 125 celery
G 125 carrot
G 125 onion
G 85 red berries
mL 100 red wine
G 250 chickpea flour
G 250 water
G 50 extra virgin olive oil
Vegetable oil for frying to taste
Salt and pepper to taste

GOAT, PRUNE
AND ALMOND TERRINE

Serves
4

Time
2 h

Calories
1028 Kcal

Wine
Marsala DOC Oro Superiore

Difficulty
Medium

Game
Goat

Chef
Dariush Lolaiy

Run
M 93' F 128'

Preparation

Cut goat meat into 1cm cubes, keep 100 g of the meat as cubes and keep 80 g of the fat as cubes. Reserve in a large mixing bowl. Mince the rest of the meat and fat together through an 8mm plate. Place half of this minced meat in the mixing bowl with the cubed meat and fat.

Put the other half back in the mincer through a 6mm mincing plate. Add this to the mixing bowl.

Gently sweat shallots, garlic, thyme, marjoram and bay in a pan on low heat.

When soft (about 10'), add brandy and sherry and cook until the brandy ignites and burns off. Add shallot mix to the mixing bowl with the parsley, prune and almonds.

Add the vinegar and season with salt and pepper, mix thoroughly to develop a sticky mixture and test-cook a little in a pan to check seasoning. The mix should taste slightly saltier than you would want, as you will be eating it at room temperature, where the salt will be less noticeable.

Line a terrine mold with a double layer of strong cling-film. Pack terrine mix very tightly into the mold. Seal with a lid or tin foil and place in a preheated 160 °C (320 °F) oven in a bain marie for about 75', the internal temperature should read 58 °C (136 °F).

Cool the terrine, and press it with a weight for at least 24 h in the fridge.

Ingredients

G 650 goat shoulder (boneless)
G 300 pork back fat (5mm cubes)
G 20 thyme
G 20 marjoram
G 100 prunes
G 100 toasted almonds, roughly chopped
mL 60 brandy
mL 40 oloroso sherry
mL 70 sherry vinegar
G 100 flat parsley
N 2 cloves garlic
N 2 shallots
N 2 bay leaves

STUFFED VENISON SAUSAGES

Serves
4

Time
30'

Calories
338 Kcal

Wine
Refosco dal Peduncolo
Rosso DOC

Difficulty
Low

Game
Deer

Chef
Villi Tosi

Run
M 31' F 42'

Preparation

Prepare the sausages by combining the venison and wild boar belly previously ground. Season with salt and pepper and knead the mixture to blend well.

Stuff the sausage mixture by first making a knot at the end of the sausage casing (already cleaned and softened), at the end of the sausage casing tie the end. Leave to rest in the fridge.

Peel and cut the potatoes carefully.

Boil them in boiling water for about 20'. When the potatoes are cooked, drain the water, add the milk and butter, and mash everything together. Use a fork to better whip the mashed potato to create a smooth, fluffy finish.

Cook the venison sausages in a skillet over medium heat or on the grill.

When they are cooked through, cut them in half, add the puree and sprinkle the cheese on top. Bake for 10' at 180 °C (356 °F) with fan assisted.

Ingredients

G 500 venison
G 300 wild boar or pork belly
G 2 pepper
G 20 salt
G 300 yellow potatoes
G 50 cheese flakes
G 20 butter
mL 75 milk
M 2 sausage casing

VENISON CAPRESE SALAD

Serves
4

Time
15'

Calories
236 Kcal

Wine
Sannio DOC Solopaca
Spumante Metodo Classico

Difficulty
Low

Game
Roe deer

Chef
Michael Hunter

Run
M 21' F 30'

Preparation

Generously season the venison with salt and pepper. Sear in a hot frying pan with a little oil on both sides 2-3' per side. Remove from the pan and rest while you prepare the salad.

Thinly slice the mozzarella and tomatoes. Slice the venison. Layer the salad with meat, tomatoes, and cheese. Generously drizzle the dish with oil, balsamic and fresh basil leaves. Sprinkle flaked sea salt to season and serve.

Ingredients

G 500 venison loin
N 2 organic tomatoes
(beef steak)
G 175 fresh mozzarella (fior di latte)
Fresh basil to taste
Sea salt to taste
Extra virgin olive oil to taste
Finishing aged balsamic to taste
Fresh crack pepper to taste

HUMMUS, CUCUMBERS
PLUM TOMATOES AND CHAMOIS

Serves
4

Time
30'

Calories
364 Kcal

Wine
Rosso Piceno DOC

Difficulty
Low

Game
Chamois

Chef
Iris Rossi

Run
M 33' F 45'

Preparation

Cut the loin into cubes of about 1 cm.

Put the chickpeas in a blender with the Tahina paste, lime juice and parsley.

Blend vigorously adding a few tablespoons of oil to make a smooth, thick mousse - add some stock if needed - and, after tasting, season with salt and pepper.

Remove the seeds from the cucumber and dice.

Clean and chop the tomatoes. Dress the cucumber and tomatoes with oil, salt, pepper and chopped chives.

Heat the oil in a frying pan over a high heat, add the coarse salt. Sear the cubed chamois loin for 1'.

Serve the hummus on the pita, arrange the cucumber and tomato salad on top and then add the cubes of chamois.

Ingredients

G 100 loin of chamois
G 250 cooked chickpeas
G 100 plum tomatoes
G 50 coarse salt
N 1 tbsp Tahina (sesame paste)
N 1 cucumber
N 1 small bunch of chives
N 2 limes, juiced
N 2 pita breads
Parsley to taste
Extra virgin olive oil to taste
Salt and pepper to taste

VENISON, BAGNA CAUDA
AND HAZELNUTS

Serves
4

Time
50'

Calories
1026 Kcal

Wine
Trentino Lagrein Riserva DOC

Difficulty
Low

Game
Roe deer

Chef
Edoardo Sbaraglia

Run
M 93' F 128'

Preparation

Trim the roe deer leg to obtain 4 pieces of about 125 g each.

For the bagna cauda, blanch the garlic in 50 g of hot milk. Repeat this process 5 times, changing the milk each time, to reduce the strength of the garlic flavor. Place the cream, capers, anchovies and blanched garlic in a small saucepan. Cook on a low heat for about 20' then blend the mixture.

To make the parsley oil, blanch the parsley leaves for 2" in boiling salted water, then plunge immediately in ice water to maintain their bright color. Take the blanched parsley and blend with the sunflower seed oil.

Sear the pieces of deer, on a hot grill, for two minutes on each side. Pour the bagna cauda onto a plate and arrange the pieces of deer on top. Season the meat with salt and pepper, add the toasted hazelnuts and dress with the parsley oil.

Ingredients

G 500 roe deer leg
G 500 fresh cream
G 250 whole milk
G 10 garlic
G 10 capers
G 60 anchovies
G 50 toasted hazelnuts
G 200 sunflower seed oil
G 50 parsley
Salt to taste
Pepper to taste

FIORDLAND WAPITI BRESAOLA

Serves
4

Difficulty
Medium

Time
1 month

Game
Elk

Calories
150 Kcal

Chef
Dariush Lolaiy

Wine
Marsala DOC Oro
Superiore Riserva

Run
M 14' F 19'

Preparation

Grind all curing ingredients in a mortar and pestle to a powder.

Rub the mix all over the meat.

Vacuum pack the meat and the cure, or place in a non-reactive container or sandwich bag, and refrigerate for 14 days, turning the meat over in the cure every few days.

Wrap the meat in a single layer of muslin cloth and hang at 12 °C (54 °F) - preferably 75% humidity - for between 2 and 8 weeks until it has lost 30% of its weight. It is important to have gentle airflow around the meat. If you don't have a suitable environment for hanging charcuterie you could use a wine chiller or your domestic fridge by using a small fan to aid in drying.

Slice thin and eat with a drizzle of good olive oil or use in a salad with rocket and pecorino cheese.

Ingredients

Kg 1,5 top round (topside)
of Fiordland Wapiti (Elk)
(substitute for wild venison)
G 37,5 kosher salt
G 30 brown sugar
G 4 curing salt
G 8 black pepper
G 3 rosemary
G 5 thyme
N 5 juniper berries

PARTRIDGE COUS COUS
WITH TURMERIC AND VEGETABLES

Serves
4

Difficulty
Low

Time
45'

Game
Partridge

Calories
318 Kcal

Chef
Iris Rossi

Wine
Etna DOC Bianco Superiore

Run
M 29' F 40'

Preparation

Take the breasts and thighs of the partridge, boil them in a vegetable stock for 30', then remove them from the pot, clean them thoroughly and fry.

Wash the vegetables and cut the zucchini, eggplant and carrots into matches, then chop the onion.

Cut the cherry tomatoes in half and set them aside.

In a pan, sauté the onion with aromatic herbs to taste, then add the other vegetables and brown them over medium heat for about 15-20', so that they become golden brown. If the bottom dries, wet with some stock. Season with salt.

Put the couscous in a bowl and cover with slightly salted boiling stock. Cover and let rest for 5', then mix it with a fork and add the turmeric.

Add the couscous with the cooked vegetables, add a drizzle of oil and the partridge meat. Serve lukewarm.

Ingredients

G 500 partridge
L 1 vegetable stock
G 140 couscous
mL 160 water
N 2 zucchini
N 1 eggplant
N 2-3 carrots
N ½ onion
N 1 tbsp turmeric
Extra virgin olive oil to taste
Salt to taste

WILD HARE
CROQUETTAS

Serves
4

Time
6 h

Calories
1033 Kcal

Wine
Verdicchio di Matelica
Riserva DOCG

Difficulty
Low

Game
Hare

Chef
Dariush Lolaiy

Run
M 93' F 128'

Preparation

Add the parsley stalks, boar hock, celery, onion, carrots, garlic, allspice berries, cloves, and bay leaves to a large casserole pot. Add enough water to submerge the hare legs so the pot is about three-quarters full. Cover with a lid and place in the oven on 160 °C (320 °F) for 4-5 h, until the meat falls away from the bone. Remove the hocks from the liquid and cool. When the meat is cool enough to handle, remove the bones. Break the meat into small pieces and set aside.

Make a roux by melting 200 g of butter in a heavy based pan. Cook 200 g flour in the butter, stirring continuously for four minutes. While whisking, add a ladle of the hare stock, repeat this process until you have used 300 ml of the cooking liquid. It should be a thick sauce resembling a bechamel. Continue to cook while stirring for another 10'. Add the mustard and ground fennel and stir to combine. Taste and adjust the seasoning with salt and black pepper to your taste. Pour the sauce into a baking tray and allow it to cool completely. When cold, mix with the meat and parsley until all ingredients are well combined.

Roll the mixture into balls, about the size of a golf ball, then shape the balls into batons. Roll in flour, then submerge in the egg whites and then roll the battens in the breadcrumbs. Fry in 170 °C (338 °F) oil, until golden. Drain on a kitchen towel, then toss in a small bowl with flaky sea salt.

Serve with mustard mayonnaise or aioli.

Ingredients

N 4 hare legs
N 1 onion, quartered
N 1 carrot, roughly chopped
N 1 stalks celery, roughly chopped
N 3 cloves garlic, chopped
N 2 shallots, peeled and finely diced
N 10 peppercorns
N 6 allspice berries
N 2 bay leaves
G 200 unsalted butter
G 400 plain flour (G 200 for pane)
G 40 dijon mustard
1 tbs ground fennel seed
N 4 egg whites lightly beaten
G 200 panko breadcrumbs
Salt and pepper to taste
Handful of chopped flat-leaf parsley
Flakey salt to serve
Mustard mayonnaise to serve

TRENTINGRANA TAGLIOLINI
VENISON STOCK AND BREAD SAUCE

Serves
4

Time
4 h

Calories
489 Kcal

Wine
Trentino Pinot Nero DOC

Difficulty
Medium

Game
Deer

Chef
Edoardo Sbaraglia

Run
M 44' F 61'

Preparation

Knead the flour with semolina, Trentingrana, egg yolks and pasta eggs. After kneading, let it rest for a couple of hours in the refrigerator covered with film. After this time, roll out the dough at approx. 5 mm.

Once the sheet has reached the right size and thickness, put it on a floured dish towel and with this help roll it up on itself. Using a long, smooth knife, slice the roll into slices of maximum 3 mm thick, sprinkle with flour and un-roll, removing excess flour.

Dry on the pin or place them on a tray covered with a floured towel so that they do not stick together.

Roast the vegetables in the oven together with the cut meat in pieces of about 4 cm x 4 cm and, when ready, transfer to a small saucepan, coat with ice and cold water and boil for about 3 h. After cooking, adjust salt and pepper.

Prepare a bread sauce by removing the outer crust of the bread, then stir-fry the bread with oil until golden brown and then add water to the brim. Cook, add herbs and mix.

Cook the tagliolini in venison stock for 3-4'.

Place the bread sauce on the bottom, add tagliolini with the venison stock and a few pieces of boiled venison and serve.

Ingredients

Kg 1 venison leg
G 200 semolina
G 140 "00" flour
G 200 egg yolk
G 50 Trentingrana cheese
G 50 egg
G 200 onions
G 200 celery
G 150 carrots
G 100 bread
G 20 extra virgin olive oil
Thyme, rosemary and sage to taste

FUSILLI WITH ROSEMARY
PHEASANT AND ORANGE ZEST

Serves
4

Time
30'

Calories
473 Kcal

Wine
Frascati Superiore DOCG

Difficulty
Low

Game
Pheasant

Chef
Roberto Dormicchi

Run
M 43' F 59'

Preparation

Cook the fusilli in plenty of salted boiling water.

In the meantime, stir-fry garlic, chopped Tropea onion and oil in a saucepan. Add the pheasant meat pounded with knife, the anchovy and the black truffle cut into cubes. Add brandy and simmer until evaporated. Season with rosemary, salt and pepper to taste.

Drain the pasta and toss with the pheasant sauce.

Serve hot, adding the orange zest.

Ingredients

G 200 pheasant meat
G 350 fusilli (spiral pasta)
N 1 anchovy
N 1 clove of garlic
N 1 orange
G 30 Tropea onion
G 50 black truffle
mL 20 brandy
Rosemary to taste
Extra virgin olive oil to taste
Salt and pepper to taste

WILD BOAR CAPPELLETTI
WITH CHEESE FONDUE, TRUFFLE AND CHERRY

Serves 4	**Time** 1 h 30'	**Calories** 700 Kcal	**Wine** Rosso Conero DOC
Difficulty High	**Game** Wild boar	**Chef** Matteo Codignoli	**Run** M 64' F 86'

Preparation

Create a volcano with flour, break the eggs and put them in the center of the volcano with a pinch of salt and oil. Beat the eggs with a fork and mix until smooth.

Cover the dough with a little oil and film, set aside for about 30'. While the dough is resting, proceed with the preparation of the filling.

Fry chopped celery, carrot, onion and rosemary in a little oil. Add the wild boar cut into cubes and brown it, shaded with red wine and cook for about 30'.

Once cooked, mince the meat, add the egg and parmesan and mix until the dough turns compact.

In a saucepan melt the butter, add the flour and stir over low heat, add the milk previously heated little by little without interruption, keeping the flame low. Complete with grated Casciotta d'Urbino cheese, nutmeg and a pinch of salt, mix very well until boiling.

Take the egg dough, remove the film and roll it with a rolling pin on a lightly floured pastry board. With the help of a bowl-dough form circles, then fill them with the filling and close them as a cappelletto.

Cook the cappelletti in salted boiling water for about 3'. Drain and sauté with melted butter and savory.

On the bottom of the plate, add a ladle of fondue, then cappelletti. Finish the dish with grated black truffle and a drizzle of black cherry syrup.

Ingredients for the filling

G 350 wild boar
N 1 carrot
N 1 onion
N 1 stalk of celery
N 1 sprig of rosemary
N 1 glass of red wine
Extra virgin olive oil to taste
Salt and pepper to taste

For the pasta dough

N 3 eggs
G 280 "0" flour
mL 1 extra virgin olive oil
Salt to taste

For the fondue

mL 400 milk
G 40 butter
G 40 "0" flour
G 100 Casciotta d'Urbino cheese
Nutmeg to taste
Black truffle to taste
Black cherry syrup to taste
Savory to taste

TORTELLI STUFFED
WITH MALLARD

Serves
4

Difficulty
Medium

Time
1 h 30'

Game
Mallard

Calories
290 Kcal

Chef
Edoardo Sbaraglia

Wine
Barbera d'Asti DOCG

Run
M 26' F 36'

Preparation

Place the grapes cut in a food bag and the sugar inside a food bag. Close the bag and leave it in the refrigerator for 5 days for the grapes to ferment.

Prepare the fresh dough by mixing the two flours with egg yolks and a pinch of salt and once the dough is made, let it rest in the refrigerator for 30' so that it rests and is easier to roll out.

While waiting, mince the mallard meat with a knife on a cutting board. Finely chop also the vegetables together with the aromatic herbs and the lard.

In a saucepan, fry the herbs and vegetables with the lard in oil. Add the mallard meat and let it brown then add the red wine and let it cook. Once the mixture is ready let it cool.

Afterwards make the tortelli pasta, rolling out the dough and cutting out the tortelli pasta with a pastry cutter; then stuff them with the previously prepared mallard.

Cook the tortelli pasta and toss them in a pan with the porcini mushrooms and herbs. Plate the tortelli pasta and add the macerated grapes and wild herbs as garnish.

Ingredients for the filling

G 250 mallard pulp
G 75 carrots
G 60 onion
G 75 celery
G 50 seasoned lard
mL 100 red wine

For the pasta

G 200 durum wheat semolina
G 100 "00" flour
N 4 egg yolks

For the dressing

G 250 grapes
G 100 wild herbs
G 125 sugar
G 100 butter
G 25 aromatic herbs
G 55 fresh porcini mushrooms
mL 75 extra virgin olive oil
Salt and pepper to taste

WILD BOAR
SPAGHETTI CARBONARA

Serves
4

Time
25'

Calories
1078 Kcal

Wine
Verdicchio dei Castelli di Jesi DOC Classico

Difficulty
Medium

Game
Wild boar

Chef
Michael Hunter

Run
M 98' F 134'

Preparation

Cut the wild boar bacon into 1-2 cm cubes and sauté in a skillet over high heat. Cook until the edges are golden brown but not completely crispy.

Add the shallot and garlic, sauté for another 2' and turn off. Cook the pasta in salted boiling water and drain it while still "al dente". Reserve 240 ml of the cooking water.

Mix the eggs and yolks with a pinch of salt and the pepper and half of the cheese. Add the pasta water to the pan with the pasta and turn on low heat. When 2/3 of the water has evaporated, turn off the heat and add the beaten eggs, stir or toss together with the bacon.

Add the rest of the cheese and continue to stir.

Distribute on plates, grate more parmesan cheese and garnish with sliced green onions.

Ingredients

G 450 wild boar bacon and pancetta
G 450 spaghetti pasta
G 75 grated parmesan cheese
G 75 grated pecorino cheese
N 3 eggs
N 3 egg yolks
N 1 minced small shallot
N 2 sliced green onions
N 2 minced cloves garlic
G 6 cracked black pepper
Salt to taste

SPELT PASTA
WITH VENISON CARBONARA

Serves
4

Time
20'

Calories
650 Kcal

Wine
Verdicchio dei Castelli di Jesi DOC Classico

Difficulty
Low

Game
Deer

Chef
Roberto Dormicchi

Run
M 59' F 81'

Preparation

Melt the butter in a non-stick frying pan and cook the venison cubes over high heat for few minutes, season with salt, pepper, marjoram.

Cook the pasta in plenty of salted water, drain and toss with the meat.

Turn of the fire, add the egg and yolks previously beaten and a little of cooking water.

Serve with grated Pecorino cheese, pepper and marjoram.

Ingredients

G 200 venison
G 400 spelt pasta
G 40 butter
G 50 Pecorino cheese
N 4 yolks
N 1 egg
Salt and pepper to taste
Marjoram to taste

PARTRIDGE AND SAVOY
CABBAGE RISOTTO

Serves
4

Difficulty
Medium

Time
30'

Game
Partridge

Calories
715 Kcal

Chef
Ilenia Rossi

Wine
Bianchello del Metauro
DOP Superiore

Run
M 65' F 90'

Preparation

Cut the partridge into approx. 2 cm pieces.

Wash and cut the cabbage into thin strips.

Make a concasse, briefly blanching the tomato in boiling water after scoring an X on its bottom with a knife. After removing the seeds, peel it before cutting it into small pieces.

Place a pan with the water on the hob and, once boiled, add the rice.

Halfway through cooking, add the partridge, cabbage and season with salt.

Once removed from the heat, add the oil and pepper, mixing well.

Serve the rice by adding the concasse seasoned beforehand with oil and salt.

Ingredients

N 2 partridges
G 320 rice
mL 600 water
G 350 savoy cabbage
mL 50 extra virgin olive oil
N 1 red tomato
N 1 pinch of black pepper
Salt to taste

CASARECCIA WITH VENISON
AND PORCINI MUSHROOMS

Serves
4

Time
50'

Calories
680 Kcal

Wine
Morellino di Scansano DOCG

Difficulty
Low

Game
Fallow deer

Chef
Edoardo Sbaraglia

Run
M 62' F 85'

Preparation

In a planetary mixer put the flours, eggs, oil and start to knead. When the mixture is well worked, add the tomato paste and continue to knead until everything is homogeneous. Let the dough rest in fridge for about 30-40'.

While waiting, cut the vegetables and the venison into cubes.

Heat the oil in a saucepan; as soon as it is hot, add the vegetables and herbs (rosemary, sage, marjoram, etc.) and let everything brown. Then add the venison meat, let it fry and at the end add the red wine. Let it cook adding some vegetable stock.

In the meantime, prepare the homemade pasta with a pasta press or make maltagliati by hand.

Next, clean the porcini mushrooms and separate the stalks from the caps. Grill the caps and cut the stalks coarsely.

When the ragù is ready, cook the pasta. In a pan with oil and rosemary, sauté the mushroom stalks and add the meat sauce. Then add the pasta and toss it all together. Stir-fry well and add the grilled mushroom caps for decoration

Ingredients for the ragù

G 350 venison meat
G 10 celery
G 15 red onions
G 10 carrots
G 35 porcini mushrooms
mL 8 red wine
Aromatic herbs to taste
Vegetable stock to taste

For the pasta

G 250 durum wheat semolina
G 200 "00" flour
G 250 egg yolk
N 1 egg
G 15 tomato concentrate
Salt to taste
Extra virgin olive oil to taste

CAPPELLACCI WITH VENISON
AND MEDITERRANEAN FLAVORS

Serves
4

Time
2 h 30'

Calories
745 Kcal

Wine
Contessa Entellina Syrah DOC

Difficulty
Medium

Game
Roe deer

Chef
Iris Rossi

Run
M 68' F 94'

Preparation

Cook the meat in a pressure cooker with the stock, red wine, onion, and carrot for around 15'.

Strain the meat and slice thinly.

Bake the whole eggplant in the oven at 190 °C (374 °F) for 1 h. Leave to cool.

Mix the meat in a bowl with the sheep's milk ricotta, Parmesan and the flesh of the eggplant.

Make the pasta dough with the flour, eggs and a pinch of salt, cover with cling film and leave it rest for 10'.

Roll out the pasta and cut into squares of around 6×6 cm. Fill the squares and seal to make the cappellacci.

Season the ricotta with salt, pepper and oil.

Cook the cappellacci in plenty of salted water, drain, then arrange in a serving dish with the diced plum tomatoes, the olives, ricotta and lemon zest. Drizzle with oil and serve.

Ingredients

G 200 venison
G 260 of "00" flour
N 3 eggs
N 1 onion
N 1 carrot
G 30 grated Parmesan cheese
mL 250 red wine
mL 250 vegetable stock
N 1 round eggplant
G 50 sheep milk ricotta
G 300 plum tomatoes
G 200 pitted Taggiasca olives
N 1 lemon
G 400 ricotta
Extra virgin olive oil to taste
Salt to taste

WILD TURKEY
AND SPRING RISOTTO

Serves 4	**Time** 30'	**Calories** 440 Kcal	**Wine** Lugana Superiore DOP
Difficulty Low	**Game** Turkey	**Chef** Michael Hunter	**Run** M 40' F 55'

Preparation

Season the turkey breast with salt and pepper. Pan sear the breast in a little oil on high heat skin side down for 2-3' per side, add your rosemary and 1 tbs 15 ml of butter.

Transfer to a 165 °C (325 °F) oven and cook for 20-25' or until internal temperature of 75 °C (145 °F).

While the turkey is cooking, puree half of the peas in a blender with a little oil. Rinse the blender and add the wild leeks and puree with a little oil.

Toast the rice on medium high heat in a medium size pot with a little olive oil until lightly golden while stirring frequently.

Add the minced shallot and garlic and sauté for 1-2'.

Add the wine and stir until absorbed.

Turn the heat to medium and slowly add the stock in stages while stirring ½ cup (125 ml) at a time. Stir until the stock is absorbed, then add more stock and cook while stirring. Continue until all the stock is absorbed.

Add 1 tsp (5 ml) of salt, add the pea and wild leek puree, remaining fresh peas, the mascarpone and parmesan cheese. Stir to incorporate.

Plate the risotto in a large bowl or plate. Slice the turkey breast. Garnish with more grated parmesan, parsley and sorrel.

Ingredients

N 1 wild turkey breast
N 1 cup (mL 250) of arborio or short grain Italian rice
N 1 small shallot
N 1 garlic clove
N 1 bunch of wild leeks
N 1.5 cups (mL 375) of fresh green sweet peas
N ½ cup (mL 125) of white wine
N 3 cups (mL 750) of chicken or turkey stock
N 1 tbs (mL 15) mascarpone
N ¼ cup (mL 60) of fresh grated parmesan cheese
N 2 rosemary sprigs
Chopped Italian parsley to taste
Wood sorrel to taste (optional)
Butter to taste
Salt and pepper to taste
Extra virgin olive oil to taste

BAKED PASTA
WITH VENISON SAUSAGE

Serves
4

Time
1 h 15'

Calories
600 Kcal

Wine
Valcalepio Rosso DOC

Difficulty
Low

Game
Deer

Chef
Villi Tosi

Run
M 55' F 75'

Preparation

In a large pan, add 25 ml of oil, add the previously diced venison sausages. Brown them and set aside, they do not need to be fully cooked.

Peel the pumpkin and potatoes and cut them into cubes of about 2 cm. Roughly chop the mushrooms after they have been cleaned. Add everything to the same pan with the chopped onion and half of the fresh herbs. Cook for 3-4' and then transfer to a large baking sheet and continue to cook for 15-20'.

In the same pan, add 25 ml of oil and add the grated zucchini, carrot, crushed garlic and remaining fresh herbs. Cook for 3-4'. Add the tomato sauce, beef stock and tomato paste. Stir, making sure everything is mixed well. Add the venison sausages and bring to a boil, then reduce the heat and simmer for 15', until the sauce has thickened.

Cook the pasta in plenty of salted water. Drain it 2' before the end of the cooking time indicated on the package. Add the pasta to the sauce. Arrange all in a baking sheet and add the mozzarella cheese. Bake in a preheated oven at 200 °C (392 °F) for 10-15'.

Ingredients

N 3 venison sausages
G 150 pumpkin
G 150 potatoes
N 4 champignon mushrooms
N 1 onion
N 1 zucchini
N 1 small carrot
G 200 chunky tomato sauce
G 30 garlic
mL 240 beef stock
N 2 tbs tomato paste
G 320 penne pasta
G 80 grated mozzarella cheese
mL 50 extra virgin olive oil
Fresh herbs (sage, thyme and rosemary) to taste
Salt and pepper to taste

WILD BOAR FAZZOLETTO

👤 **Serves**
4

⏱ **Time**
8 h 30'

🔥 **Calories**
440 Kcal

🍷 **Wine**
Chianti Classico DOCG

⭐ **Difficulty**
Medium

🦌 **Game**
Wild boar

👤 **Chef**
Dariush Lolaiy

🏃 **Run**
M 40' F 55'

Preparation

Brown the meat in a hot pan to caramelize the meat. Remove the meat from the pan when you have a golden brown color. Slice the onion and the garlic, cook them in the same pan with a little oil. When the onions are softened, cut the tomatoes in half and add them in the pan. Cook until charred.

Add the wine and stock, return the meat to the liquid and braise at 120 °C (248 °F) for 8 h. Remove the cooked meat and vegetables from the liquid and shred the meat. Reduce the liquid by half to concentrate the flavor. Add the meat and vegetables back to the reduced liquid.

Sift the flour and semolina (15 g) onto a clean, dry bench top. Mix the eggs and pour them into the center of the well, then slowly incorporate the flour into the egg mixture, until you have a ball of dough. Cover it with cling film and rest for 10'.

Roll out the pasta with a rolling pin, then pass it through your pasta machine and repeat the operation until obtaining a 3mm fillo dough. Cut the pasta into 20 cm sheets and layer one on top of the other, dusting with semolina between each sheet.

In salted boiling water, cook the fresh pasta "al dente". Add the pasta to the ragù and toss in the pan for 1' to thicken the sauce. Add oil, chopped mint and Parmesan. Serve with extra Parmesan, salt, pepper and chopped chives.

Ingredients

G 600 wild boar shoulder
N 2 onions
N 4 cloves garlic
G 500 ripe tomatoes
mL 150 red wine
mL 300 boar or chicken stock
G 140 "00" flour
G 15 superfine semolina
N 2 egg yolks
N 1 whole egg
N 2 tbsp chives
G 150 Parmesan cheese
Mint to taste
Extra virgin olive oil to taste

CAPPELLACCI PASTA
WITH PHEASANT, PEPPERS AND CRUSCO

👤 **Serves** 4	⏲ **Time** 4 h	🔥 **Calories** 1305 Kcal
⭐ **Difficulty** Medium	🦌 **Game** Pheasant	👤 **Chef** Edoardo Sbaraglia

🍷 **Wine** F.V.G. Cabernet Sauvignon DOC

🏃 **Run** M 118' F 163'

Preparation

For the pasta, combine all the ingredients until you get a smooth and homogeneous dough and let it rest in the refrigerator.

For the pheasant sauce, mince the pheasant meat in a mincer. Cut the vegetables into small cubes and brown them in the melted lard in a frying pan. Add the minced pheasant and allow to brown, add the wine and when almost evaporated add the water and cook for about 1 h 30'. Once cooked, allow to cool.

For the yellow pepper cream, heat the oil, add the deseeded and cubed peppers, add the water and allow to cook. Season to taste with salt and blend.

For the red pepper stock, put the sliced peppers in a saucepan with cold water and cook for 2 h on a low heat. After 2 h, blend and filter. Now roll out the pasta dough to a thickness of 6 mm, cut out rounds with a pastry cutter and stuff with the pheasant sauce and seal to form the cappellacci.

Cook the cappellacci in boiling salted water, drain and mix with the yellow pepper cream.

Arrange in a serving dish, pour over the cold red pepper stock and garnish with the fresh oregano and crumbled crusco pepper.

Ingredients for the ragù

G 800 pheasant meat
G 100 carrots
G 150 onions
G 150 celery
G 100 white wine
G 100 lard

For the pasta

G 400 "00" flour
G 100 semolina
G 220 egg yolk
N 1 egg

For the yellow bell pepper cream

G 500 yellow bell peppers
G 30 extra virgin olive oil
G 7 salt

For the red bell pepper stock

G 700 red bell pepper
mL 1300 water
G 10 crusco pepper
G 4 oregano

FISARMONICHE, MOUFLON
SMALL MEATBALLS AND EGGPLANTS

Serves
4

Time
30'

Calories
228 Kcal

Wine
A.A. Lagrein DOC

Difficulty
Medium

Game
Mouflon

Chef
Roberto Dormicchi

Run
M 21' F 29'

Preparation

Combine the mouflon meat, the egg, the Parmesan, the chopped marjoram, salt and pepper. Shape into meatballs. Cook in a pan with a little oil, salt and pepper.

Make a cross cut on top of ripe tomatoes, blanch them in boiling water, cool in water and ice. Peel them and remove the seeds, cut them into cubes and toss with oil, salt and pepper.

Cut the eggplants into sticks, add salt and pepper. Cook in oven at 170 °C (338 °F) for about 7'. Add a little oil, salt and set aside.

Cook the pasta in plenty of salted boiling water, drain "al dente" and toss with the tomatoes and the meatballs.

Serve the pasta with the eggplant sticks and the ricotta pressed through a potato ricer.

Ingredients

G 150 mouflon ground meat
G 350 Fisarmoniche pasta
N 1 egg
G 15 Parmesan cheese
G 200 ripe tomatoes
G 100 eggplants
G 100 ricotta
Marjoram to taste
Extra virgin olive oil to taste
Salt and pepper to taste

SPAGHETTI WITH GAME RAGÙ
AND BURRATA

👤 **Serves**
4

🐢 **Time**
45'

⛰ **Calories**
844 Kcal

🍷 **Wine**
Campi Flegrei DOC
Piedirosso

☆ **Difficulty**
Low

🦌 **Game**
Mixed

👨‍🍳 **Chef**
Michael Hunter

🏃 **Run**
M 76' F 105'

Preparation

Preheat a large pot on high heat, add a tablespoon of oil. Add the ground game meat with a pinch of salt and pepper. Let the meat caramelize before stirring with a wooden spoon.

Once browned add the shallot finely diced and the minced garlic and stir occasionally for 2-3'.

Deglaze the pot by adding the white wine and stirring. Cook off the alcohol for 2' then add the thyme previously chopped, chili flakes, stock and tomato puree.

Turn down the heat to low/medium and simmer for 30-40'.

Fill a large pot with water and add a tablespoon of salt to season. Heat on high to boil.

When the sauce is done, add the pasta to the boiling water and cook to "al dente", drain the pasta reserving a cup of the pasta water.

Toss the pasta with the pasta sauce, adding a little of the pasta water to adjust consistency, grate some fresh Parmesan on top with a little oil. Taste for seasoning and add a pinch of salt.

Chop the fresh basil and oregano, plate the pasta, garnish with a half ball of the burrata cheese, sprinkling with the fresh herbs and a pinch of flaked sea salt.

Ingredients

G 450 ground venison
G 200 ground wild boar
(fatty cuts if possible)
G 500 (2 balls) burrata cheese
N 2 shallots
N 4 cloves of garlic
N 2 sprigs of thyme leaves
N 2 sprigs of fresh oregano
N 4 sprigs of fresh basil leaves
N ½ teaspoon chili flakes
mL 500 dark beef or game stock
L 1 tomato sauce
mL 250 white wine
N 2 tbsp extra virgin olive oil
Parmesan cheese to taste
Coarse salt to taste
Salt and pepper to taste

RISOTTO WITH CHICORY
AND HARE

Serves
4

Time
30'

Calories
480 kcal

Wine
Gavi DOCG

Difficulty
Medium

Game
Hare

Chef
Roberto Dormicchi

Run
M 43' F 60'

Preparation

Cook the hare meat in a pan with oil, garlic, rosemary and sage.

Add brandy and flame. Add salt and pepper to taste.

In saucepan, stir-fry the anchovy, oil and the chicory already boiled, dried and chopped. Season with salt and pepper to taste.

Toast the rice and add stock little by little, at 3/4 of cooking time add the hare meat combined with lemon zest, parmesan and butter.

Serve accompanied with some sautéed chicory.

Ingredients

G 150 pounded hare meat
G 300 Carnaroli rice
G 900 stock
G 50 chicory
G 30 butter
G 30 Parmesan cheese
mL 20 brandy
N 1 clove of garlic
N 1 anchovy
Rosemary and sage to taste
Lemon zest to taste
Extra virgin olive oil to taste
Salt and pepper to taste

HERB CRUSTED VENISON
CROWN ROAST

Serves
4

Time
1 h

Calories
226 Kcal

Wine
Sforzato di Valtellina DOCG

Difficulty
Medium

Game
Roe deer

Chef
Wade Truong

Run
M 20' F 28'

Preparation

Preheat the oven to 350 °C (662 °F) and french, tie the venison rack.

Preheat a heavy bottomed pan to high heat.

Season the rack with salt and pepper, and sear on all sides in a heavy bottomed pan. Remove from the pan and allow to cool for 1' or 2'.

Brush the rack with beaten egg white (try to not get any on the bones) and cover with minced herbs. Tie the rack into a circle (crown) with the rib bones arching outwards. Place back in the heavy bottomed pan and roast for 15-30' until the internal temperature is 50 °C (120 °F).

Remove from the oven, and remove the rack from the pan. Allow it to rest for 10-15'. Internal temperature should rest up to 52-55 °C (125-130 °F) for a solid medium rare.

Cut the twine, carve, and serve.

Ingredients

N 1 bone in rack of venison
N 1 bunch of fresh thyme
N 1 bunch of fresh rosemary
N 1 egg white, beaten

CHAMOIS CUTLETS

 Serves
4

 Time
30'

Calories
856 Kcal

 **Wine**
Valle d'Aosta DOC Nebbiolo

Difficulty
Medium

Game
Chamois

Chef
Ilenia Rossi

Run
M 78' F 107'

Preparation

Pound the slices of chamois with a meat tenderizer.

Beat the eggs in a bowl.

Dredge each slice in the flour, then dip in the beaten egg and coat in the breadcrumbs.

Press the meat into the breadcrumbs to make sure it is fully coated.

Heat the butter in a small frying pan until it reaches 169 °C (336 °F), add the cutlets and fry until golden on both sides.

Place on paper towels to drain and season with salt. Serve hot with your favorite sides.

Ingredients

G 600 slices of chamois
(about 3cm thick)
G 120 white flour
N 3 eggs
G 400 breadcrumbs
G 400 clarified butter
Salt to taste

ELK CHILI

Serves
4

Time
40'

Calories
300 Kcal

Wine
Primitivo di Manduria DOC

Difficulty
Low

Game
Elk

Chef
Michael Hunter

Run
M 27' F 37'

Preparation

Preheat a medium-sized skillet over high heat and add a little oil, celery, onion, and garlic and brown the sauté. Add the venison and add salt and pepper to taste. Let it fry for 3-4' before stirring to caramelize and brown the meat.

Stir and let cook completely while stirring.

Add the spices, tomato puree, beans, and stock.

Cook for 25-30' over medium heat in a semi-covered pot with a lid.

Serve the chili hot with the optional garnish immediately or cool and refrigerate for up to 1 week. The chili can be reheated and packed into a thermos for your hunting trip.

Ingredients

G 500 minced elk meat
G 750 tomato sauce
N 1 diced small onion
N 4 minced cloves garlic
N 2 diced stalks of celery
G 18 canned kidney beans
(white or red)
mL 250 stock (game or beef)
G 5 ground cumin
G 30 chili powder
G 5 chili flakes
G 5 cayenne pepper
Salt and pepper to taste
Extra virgin olive oil to taste

Optional garnish

Sliced green onion to taste
Sliced Jalapeño peppers to taste
Chopped cilantro to taste
Sour cream to taste
Grated cheddar cheese to taste

HARE'S STEW

Serves
4

Time
2 h 30'

Calories
250 Kcal

Wine
Ischia DOC Piedirosso

Difficulty
Medium

Game
Hare

Chef
Edoardo Sbaraglia

Run
M 23' F 31'

Preparation

Clean and peel the red turnip and let them season in raspberry vinegar overnight. Dry the Taggiasca olives in oven at 50 °C (122 °F) overnight, or in a microwave for 5' and pass them through a cutter.

Remove the loin from the bone-in saddle and cut it into fillets.

Toast the hare's bones in the oven and then transfer them to a saucepan and fry them with celery, carrot, and onion, simmering with red wine. As soon as the wine has evaporated, cover everything with cold water and let it cook until the mixture is reduced. At this point, filter through a sieve and let it rest in the fridge for 2 h.

Remove the fat from the top of the pan to obtain the hare's stock.

Clean the chard, sauté in a hot pan and adjust the salt. Sear the hare fillets in a pan with oil and rosemary.

Serve the fillets on the chard with the baby carrots and the red turnip, then place the Taggiasca olives around them. Before serving the dish pour a little of game stock on the hare.

Ingredients

G 600 hare bone-in saddle
G 80 Taggiasca olives
G 125 baby carrots
G 100 Swiss chard
G 50 celery
G 50 carrot
G 50 onion
N 4 red turnip
Raspberry vinegar to taste
Red wine to taste
Rosemary to taste
Salt and pepper to taste
Extra virgin olive oil to taste

VENISON TOMAHAWK
WITH FLORETS SALAD

SECOND COURSE

👤 **Serves**
4

⏱ **Time**
30'

🔥 **Calories**
348 Kcal

🍷 **Wine**
Vino Nobile
di Montepulciano DOCG

⭐ **Difficulty**
Low

🦌 **Game**
Roe deer

👨‍🍳 **Chef**
Iris Rossi

🏃 **Run**
M 31' F 43'

Preparation

Finely chop the herbs with the pink peppercorns. Rub the ribs with this mixture.

Cook the broccoli and cauliflower florets in a saucepan with plenty of salted water for 5'. Cool in cold water. Dress the florets with the anchovy dripping.

Cook the meat in a grill pan with oil and coarse salt.

Arrange the ribs on a serving dish with the floret salad and drizzle with olive oil.

Ingredients

N 8 venison ribs
N 1 Romanesco broccoli
N 1 orange cauliflower
Anchovy dripping to taste
Pink peppercorns to taste
Rosemary and thyme to taste
Extra virgin olive oil to taste
Salt to taste

VENISON TARTARE
WITH OCTOBER SCENT

Serves
4

Time
50'

Calories
385 Kcal

Wine
Collio Sauvignon DOC

Difficulty
Low

Game
Deer

Chef
Ilenia Rossi

Run
M 35' F 50'

Preparation

Remove all the ribbing and skin from the venison fillet. Mince the meat with a knife to obtain small cubes.

Season the minced meat with chopped spring onion, caper, Worcestershire sauce, chili, truffles, salt and pepper.

Grate 100 g truffle and add it to the sour cream along with oil, salt and pepper to taste.

Clean the porcini mushrooms and cut them into thin slices.

Put the cream on a plate, add the tartare, place the egg yolk on top of the meat and finish garnishing with porcini mushrooms and grated truffle.

Ingredients

Kg 1 venison fillet
N 1 spring onion
N 4 quail egg yolks
N 8 capers
G 180 sour cream
G 200 black truffle
G 100 porcini mushrooms
Worcestershire sauce to taste
Mustard to taste
Chili to taste (optional)
Salt and pepper to taste
Extra virgin olive oil to taste

WILD BOAR
BBQ RIBS

Serves
4

Time
3 h

Calories
255 Kcal

Wine
Rosso di Montepulciano DOC

Difficulty
Medium

Game
Wild boar

Chef
Michael Hunter

Run
M 23' F 32'

Preparation

Mix all of the spices to evenly combine. Brush the ribs with the maple syrup and season with all the dry rub, salt, and pepper.

Let the ribs flavor over night if desired or start your smoker or oven and preheat to 125 °C (257 °F) place the ribs inside and cook to internal temperature of 70 °C (158 °F) for about 1 h.

Wrap the ribs in foil or butcher paper and continue cooking until 90 °C (194 °F) internal temperature about another 1/1 h 30'. At this temperature the meat should be able to easily be pulled apart.

Let the ribs rest for 15' covered before slicing. The drippings can be brushed on or add your favorite barbecue sauce. Garnish with chopped fresh coriander and green onion.

Ingredients

N 2 full racks of wild boar ribs
mL 125 maple syrup
G 100 paprika
G 15 garlic powder
G 15 onion powder
G 5 cayenne pepper
G 5 ground coriander
G 15 salt
G 5 ground black pepper
Fresh coriander to taste
Green onion to taste

WOOD PIGEON, CHICORY
RED FRUIT APPLES AND HAZELNUT SAUCE

Serves
4

Time
60'

Calories
525 Kcal

Wine
Candia dei Colli Apuani
DOC Vermentino Nero

Difficulty
Medium

Game
Wood pigeon

Chef
Edoardo Sbaraglia

Run
M 48' F 66'

Preparation

Wash the red fruits and blend them cold with an immersion blender, then filter skins and seeds, if present.

For the hazelnut sauce, add two parts of the cooking juice with a part of the hazelnut paste and mix well together.

Then make the anchovy emulsion by mixing in a glass anchovies, lemon, oil, salt, pepper and garlic and blend everything together.

Then clean the cicoria asparago from the outer leaves, cut them in halves and leave them to soak in cold water and ice. Blanch the leaves in salted water for 1', cool them quickly in water and ice and then blend and season with oil, salt and pepper.

Take the whole pigeon and season it lightly with salt also on the side of the carcass. In a frying pan with oil, lightly cook it over low heat on the side of the breast until the skin is crisp. Remove the sides to facilitate the cooking of the legs. Finish cooking in the oven at 200 °C (392 °F) for 2'.

Pour the cicoria asparago leaves sauce on a flat plate randomly using a spoon. Season the cicoria asparago with the anchovy emulsion and place them in the center of the dish. Cut the apple into matchsticks and season it with salt, pepper and red fruit sauce and then arrange them on the plate. Draw the pigeon's breast and legs and place them on the plate. Season the whole with the hazelnut sauce.

Ingredients

G 570 wood pigeon
G 130 apples
G 95 red fruit mix
G 175 cicoria asparago
G 130 cicoria asparago leaves
G 30 anchovies
G 15 lemon
mL 80 extra virgin olive oil
G 5 rosemary, sage, thyme, garlic
G 25 hazelnut paste
G 75 cooking juice
Salt to taste
Pepper to taste

SIKA CARPACCIO

Serves
4

Time
50'

Calories
528 Kcal

Wine
A.A. Spumante Rosè DOC

Difficulty
Low

Game
Deer

Chef
Wade Truong

Run
M 48' F 66'

Preparation

Ground fine dried porcini mushrooms into a coarse powder.

Season the backstrap liberally with salt and pepper, then dust with porcini mushrooms powder.

Heat a wide, heavy-bottomed pan to high heat with a little cooking oil or fat (reserve the oil for serving). Quickly sear the backstrap, just long enough to add a little color, 15-20", on all sides.

After searing, place the backstrap in the freezer for 20-40'. You want it almost frozen, to make it easier to slice thinly and pound.

Remove the almost-frozen meat from the freezer and slice across the grain, 1/3" thick. Place the slices on a cutting board. At this point, you can layer the slices between two pieces of plastic wrap if you choose - this reduces potential splatter and allows you to easily peel the meat up off the board without tearing it. Use a meat mallet to pound the slices as thin as possible (almost translucent) without completely tearing the meat apart. Gentle, steady motion is what you're looking for here. Remember, the meat is already sliced thin, so there is no need to go full caveman at this point.

Once the meat has been hammered out, transfer it to a large plate, then season with olive oil, salt, capers and slices of good Parmesan.

Ingredients

G 600 venison backstrap (Sika deer)
G 100 salt packed capers
G 120 shaved thin Parmesan cheese
G 80 dried porcini mushrooms
Salt to taste
Extra virgin olive oil to taste

VENISON PASTRAMI
CHAMOMILE MAYONNAISE, PICKLED CHERRIES

Serves
4

Time
50'

Calories
893 Kcal

Wine
Trentino Lagrein DOC

Difficulty
Medium

Game
Fallow deer

Chef
Edoardo Sbaraglia

Run
M 81' F 111'

Preparation

Place all the ingredients for the brine in a saucepan - water, salt (200 g), sugar (183 g), cane sugar (60 g), honey, cinnamon, cloves (2 g) and black pepper (3 g) - bring to the boil then leave to cool. Once cold, place the venison leg in the brine and leave for 24 h.

For the mayonnaise, whisk the egg yolks, adding the vegetable oil a little at a time, add the salt (3 g) and lemon juice, then blend with the chamomile.

For the pop-amaranth, heat a frying pan and pour the amaranth seeds in a few seeds at a time, after a few seconds they will start to pop like popcorn, remove immediately from the heat and place in a cold dish.

For the pickled cherries wash and stone the cherries. Put cloves (2 g), star anise, raspberry vinegar, apple vinegar and cane sugar (80 g) in a saucepan, bring to the boil, allow to cool for 5' and then pour over the stoned cherries.

Take the leg out of the brine and rub it with the spice mix - combining black pepper (20 g), coriander seeds, mustard seeds, fennel seeds and smoked paprika - cook at 90 °C (194 °F) until the temperature reaches 50 °C (122 °F) at the core. Slice the meat very thinly and arrange on the serving dish, add some small mounds of chamomile mayonnaise, the cherries and 3 level tablespoons of pop-amaranth.

Ingredients

Kg 1 venison leg
G 70 amaranth seeds
L 3 water
G 183 sugar
G 140 cane sugar
G 50 honey
G 23 black pepper
G 15 coriander seeds
G 25 mustard seeds
G 5 fennel seeds
G 5 smoked paprika
N 2 egg yolks
mL 250 vegetable oil
G 60 cherries
G 4 cloves
G 1 star anise
G 200 raspberry vinegar
G 200 apple cider vinegar
G 203 salt
mL 6 lemon juice
G 5 chamomile
G 2 cinnamon

VENISON BURGERS
WITH POPLARS

Serves
4

Time
20'

Calories
500 Kcal

Wine
Colli Maceratesi
DOC Rosso

Difficulty
Low

Game
Deer

Chef
Iris Rossi

Run
M 45' F 62'

Preparation

Prepare the burgers by combining the venison meat and the ground bacon, add marjoram, breadcrumbs and Parmesan. Season with salt and pepper.

Form four balls of equal size with the minced meat and make 4 hamburgers.

Heat a frying pan over high heat, add the butter and cook the previously cleaned poplars, adding a little water and the chopped marjoram. Season with salt and pepper.

Cook the meat for about 4' per side, until you get a well browned surface.

Remove from the frying pan and place on the serving dish together with the poplars.

Ingredients

G 400 minced venison meat
G 150 ground rolled bacon
G 50 Parmesan cheese
G 50 breadcrumbs
G 200 poplar mushrooms (poplars)
G 30 butter
Marjoram to taste
Extra virgin olive oil to taste
Salt and pepper to taste

CAPERCAILLIE WITH POTATOES
ONION CREAM AND BLUEBERRY SAUCE

Serves
4

Time
45'

Calories
445 Kcal

Wine
Cirò DOC Rosso Classico

Difficulty
High

Game
Capercaillie

Chef
Gabriel Jonsson

Run
M 40' F 55'

Preparation

Put 450 g of the butter in a saucepan together with the small yellow onions and the potatoes, a few sprigs of rosemary and thyme and 3 crushed cloves of garlic. Cook on medium heat until the potatoes are completely soft.

Pick up the potatoes and let the onions continue to jam until completely soft. Take the onions and let them cool. Mix them together with the egg yolk and add a little of the melted butter. Season with salt and pepper.

Heat a frying pan with rapeseed oil. Salt the meat and brown it on both sides. Lower the heat and add 50 g butter, herbs and 1 clove of garlic. Spoon the capercaillie with the butter.

Place the bird in the oven at 150 °C (302 °F) to an internal temperature of 53 °C (127 °F). Let rest for at least 5' before serving.

Add a little more butter to the frying pan you just fried the capercaillie in with the chopped shallots. Add wine, 80 ml game stock, gin and some junipers. Let this reduce for 20', strain and reduce to the desired consistency and taste. Butter the sauce just before serving and add the blueberries.

In a frying pan, heat the confit butter, previously set aside, removing the red onions and add the chanterelles. Once half-cooked, add the small red onions as well. Put in the confit potatoes and let it get color. Pour in 1 tablespoon of the sauce and the remaining game stock. Serve the meat with potatoes and blueberry sauce.

Ingredients

N 1 capercaillie breast
N 16 small potatoes
N 10 small yellow onions
(or N 4 large ones)
N 8 small red onions
G 200 chanterelles
N 4 garlic cloves
G 500 butter
dL 4 red wine
N 2 tbsp gin
dL 1 game stock
N 1 shallot
N 1 pot of thyme
N 1 jar of rosemary
N 1 egg yolk
N 10 junipers
dL 1 frozen blueberries
Rapeseed oil to taste
Salt and pepper to taste

CRISPY HARE CONFIT

Serves
4

Time
2 h 15'

Calories
290 Kcal

Wine
Etna DOC Rosato

Difficulty
Medium

Game
Hare

Chef
Wade Truong

Run
M 25' F 35'

Preparation

Combine sugar and salt and use it to season the meat. Wrap and refrigerate overnight.

Preheat the oven to 135 °C (275 °F). Rinse the hare with cold water and pat dry. Place in Dutch oven with all the spices. Pour in oil until the meat is submerged. Cover with lid and place on the middle rack of the oven for 2-3 h until fork tender but not quite falling off the bone.

Allow to cool in the oil (confit is always better when it cools in the fat). You can refrigerate the entire thing for a couple of days or get right to finishing it.

Preheat broiler. Strain hare from oil (save the oil to roast vegetables, make croutons, or dip bread) and place on a sheet pan and broil for 2-3' until crispy, then flip and cook the other side for 2-3'.

Serve with crusty bread and roasted vegetables or shred it and add to soups or salads.

Ingredients

N 1 hare, quarters, and chopped loins
G 50 salt
G 20 sugar
G 20 mustard seed
N 4 cloves garlic
N 2 bay leaves
G 3 whole clove
G 20 whole peppercorn
N 4 pods star anise
G 20 whole green cardamom
N 4-5 sprigs thyme
N 3 sprigs rosemary
Extra virgin olive oil to taste

SALMI OF DUCK

Serves 4	**Time** 15 h	**Calories** 846 Kcal	**Wine** Barbaresco DOCG
Difficulty Low	**Game** Duck	**Chef** Edoardo Sbaraglia	**Run** M 77' F 106'

Preparation

Place the duck carcasses with the red wine, juniper, black pepper and cloves to marinate for 12 h.

Then roast the bones in the oven at 200 °C (392 °F) for about 30'. Put some oil and the sliced vegetables in a saucepan and sauté until nicely colored. When the vegetables are nicely sauteed, add the carcasses and the wine previously used to marinate the meat, and allow to boil for about 3 h. Strain the mixture and reduce it to 1/3.

Take the duck thighs, season them with salt and pepper and cook them in a vacuum pouch for 12 h at 78 °C (172 °F), alternatively cook in a static oven at 160 °C (320 °F) for about 40'. Once cooked, pull the meat from the thighs and place on a sheet of brik paper lightly brushed with egg, then roll it all up to form a cylinder.

Take a cold frying pan and place the duck breasts in it, skin side down, place over a low flame and allow to cook until the skin becomes a nice brown color, finish cooking in the oven at 200 °C (392 °F) for 5'.

Lightly sear the mixed leaves with oil and season with salt and pepper.

Fry the previously prepared cylinders and once ready cut them in half. Cut the duck breasts in half too and arrange on the plate along with the brik pastry cylinders, place the stirred-fry mixed leaves in the center. Drench with the salmi sauce.

Ingredients

G 600 duck breast
G 200 duck thighs
L 1 red wine
Kg 1 duck carcasses
G 400 of mixed salad leaves
N 10 juniper berries
N 10 black peppercorns
N 4 cloves
G 200 onion
G 200 carrot
G 200 celery
G 70 brik pastry sheets (about 4)
G 20 extra virgin olive oil

TEMPURA TURKEY TENDERS
WITH PONZU

Serves
4

Difficulty
Low

Time
20'

Game
Turkey

Calories
437 Kcal

Chef
Wade Troung

Wine
Trebbiano d'Abruzzo
Superiore DOC

Run
M 39' F 55'

Preparation

Mix seasoning ingredients, set aside. Mix ponzu sauce ingredients, stir until sugar is dissolved.

Remove tendon from tenders. Cut tenders in half lengthwise and tenderize with a mallet until ¼ thick. Mix with seasoning and refrigerate for 2-4 h.

Preheat frying oil to 180 °C (356 °F).

Mix tempura batter with chopsticks or fork. Stir lightly- overmixing will cause the gluten to bind and create a "doughy" batter. There will be clumps in the batter, this is normal. Keep the batter cold until use.

Remove tenders from seasoning and shake off excess. Dip in tempura batter and fry for 2-4' until just golden brown. Work in small batches and allow oil to heat back up before frying another batch. Rest cooked tenders on a wire rack or paper towel lined plate.

Serve hot with ponzu.

Ingredients

N 2 turkey tenders

For the seasoning

mL 40 soy sauce
mL 40 sake
G 10 minced ginger
G 5 minced garlic

For the tempura batter

G 50 flour
G 50 potato starch
mL 250 water
N 1 egg

For the ponzu sauce

mL 80 soy sauce
mL 50 yuzu juice (or lemon juice)
mL 15 rice wine vinegar
G 15 sugar

ROASTED VENISON
WITH BÉRNAISE SAUCE

Serves
4

Time
45'

Calories
350 Kcal

Wine
Valcalepio rosso DOC

Difficulty
Low

Game
Deer

Chef
Michael Hunter

Run
M 31' F 43'

Preparation

Season the venison with salt and pepper. Preheat a large cast iron or heavy bottomed skillet, add oil and sear venison for 2-3' or until golden brown. Turn, add the butter and thyme to the pan. Transfer to the oven at 150 °C (302 °F) and bake until the internal temperature is 50 °C (122 °F) for medium rare. Let rest for 10' before slicing. While the venison is almost ready to cook, start the Béarnaise sauce.

Heat the butter to separate the fat from the milk (microwave or in a saucepan) and set aside. Add the egg yolks, wine, salt and pepper to a medium bowl. Whisk vigorously over a pot of boiling water (over medium-low heat) until the egg is foamy and holds a ribbon (ribbon stage) this is when the heat has thickened the egg and the whisking has added air to make it fluffy.

Do not boil the water over high heat underneath because the eggs may scramble. Remove from the heat and slowly whisk in the melted butter. Add the lemon juice and chopped tarragon.

If the sauce is too thick or splits, add a tablespoon or two of the hot water from the pot and whisk to bring together or adjust the consistency. Adjust salt if necessary.

Slice the venison and pour the sauce over it. Serve with seasonal vegetables.

Ingredients

Kg 1 venison loin
Butter to taste
Thyme to taste
Salt and pepper to taste
Extra virgin olive oil to taste

For the Béarnaise sauce

N 4 egg yolks
G 175 butter
N 1 lemon
G 30 tarragon
mL 30 white wine
Salt and pepper to taste

WILD BOAR TENDERLOIN
WITH SQUASH, APPLES AND BLACK KALE

👤 **Serves**
4

⏲ **Time**
1 h 30'

🔥 **Calories**
600 Kcal

🍷 **Wine**
Chianti Rufina DOCG

⭐ **Difficulty**
Low

🦌 **Game**
Wild boar

👤 **Chef**
Michael Hunter

🏃 **Run**
M 55' F 75'

Preparation

Cut the squash in halt removing the bottom round part with the seeds. Cut the seed part of the squash in half and scoop out the seeds and discard. Place on a baking sheet and roast at 200 °C (400 °F) skin side up.

While the squash is cooking add the stock and cream to a pot and bring to a simmer. Once the squash halves are soft remove from the oven and peel off the skin. Add the squash to the pot of cream and stock and cook for 5'. Add a pinch of salt and butter. Blend it all together.

Meanwhile, peel the remaining half squash with a peeler and cut into 6mm round slices. Place the squash slices on a baking tray, brush with oil and season with salt and pepper and add to the oven. Cook for 15-20' or until soft.

Pre heat a heavy pan on high heat. Season the boar tenderloin with salt and pepper. Add a splash of oil to the pan and sear the meat for 2-3' on either side. Transfer to the oven and cook for 5-10' depending on your desired doneness. Rest for 5' before slicing.

Slice half the apple into round slices and dice the other half. Add the diced apple to a bowl and add the lemon juice, mustard, sliced green onion and a pinch of salt and pepper. Stir to combine and set aside.

Sauté the kale in a little oil. Add a pinch of salt and pepper. Crush the garlic and add to the pan. Cook for 2-3' or until the kale has wilted.

Add the purée to the plate first, then the kale. Slice the tenderloin and arrange on top. Add the sliced apple and sliced squash beside the tenderloin and spoon the diced apple over top.

Ingredients

N 2 whole wild boar tenderloins
N 1 large butternut squash
N 2 large apple
N 1 bunch of black kale
N 1 bunch of green onion sliced
G 15 butter
N 1 tbsp grain mustard
mL 240 chicken beef or game stock
mL 120 cream
N 1 lemon juiced
N 1 clove of garlic
Salt and pepper to taste
Extra virgin olive oil to taste

AIR COMPRESSED
ROASTED DUCK

Serves
4

Time
50'

Calories
422 Kcal

Wine
Cerasuolo d'Abruzzo DOC

Difficulty
Low

Game
Duck

Chef
Wade Truong

Run
M 40' F 50'

Preparation

Take a whole, skin-on bird and using the compressor and a blowgun nozzle, force air under the skin. The duck will inflate like a beach ball and the skin will stretch out. Wear eye protection while you do this.

Work around the bird and get air under all the skin. The skin should look a little baggy when you're done. Place the bird on a rack or hang in the refrigerator for a day or two to allow the skin to dry out.

When you're ready to cook, preheat the oven to 190° C (375 °F). Season the bird with salt and pepper and place on an elevated roasting rack in a pan. Roast for 10'.

All ovens are different, and ducks vary in size, so keep an eye on the bird as it is roasting. You are not trying to cook the bird in the first 2 stages as much as you are trying to render some of the fat off the skin.

Remove from the oven and tilt the bird to allow fat to drain. Allow to cool down for around 15'. Put the duck back in the oven and roast for another 10', remove and allow to drain again. Allow to cool for around 15'.

Turn the oven up to 210 °C (425 °F) and roast for 5-10' until the thickest part of the breast hits 55 °C (130 °F). Remove from the oven and allow to drain.

In a saucepan, heat 2-3 cups of canola or similar oil to 190° C (375°F). With the bird on a roasting rack over the roasting pan, carefully ladle the hot oil over the bird. Keep doing this over the entire bird, allowing each area to cool down a bit before ladling more oil onto it. One the skin is crispy and amber brown, carve it up and serve with your favorite sides.

Ingredients

1 duck
G 150 canola or similar oil
Salt and pepper to taste

ACKNOWLEDGEMENTS

Hold on one more minute! We know that after a quick look at the wonderful dishes our chefs presented you can't wait to run into the kitchen, put on your apron and have fun playing the flavors and colors that fill these pages.

But first allow us a few more lines to thank everyone who have made possible the creation of this third volume of recipes and who with passion and enthusiasm promote and support the Franchi Food Academy project, in which taste and sustainability go hand in hand.

A path started as a game more than 7 years ago that has now become an opportunity to meet, share ideas, synergies and flavors, thanks to all the people who are now part of it. Do you want to get on board too?

Send your recipe to **foodacademy@franchi.com**, you could become the next Franchi Food Academy Chef!

#TASTERIGHT

Made and produced in Italy
Printing closed in December 2022

marettimanfrediedizioni.it
Instagram: marettimanfrediedizioni
Facebook: Maretti e Manfredi Edizioni